Safety First

Be safe!

Weather Safety

STORM ALERT

childsworld.com

BY SUSAN KESSELRING

ILLUSTRATED BY DAN McGEEHAN

T0407288

Published by The Child's World®
800-599-READ · childsworld.com

Copyright © 2025 by The Child's World®
All rights reserved. No part of this book may be reproduced or utilized in any form or by any means without written permission from the publisher.

Photo Credit:
© Mary Swensen: 22

ISBN Information
9781503894044 (Reinforced Library Binding)
9781503895126 (Portable Document Format)
9781503895942 (Online Multi-user eBook)
9781503896765 (Electronic Publication)

LCCN
2024942722

Printed in the United States of America

ABOUT THE AUTHOR

Susan Kesselring loves children, books, nature, and her family. She teaches K-1 students in a progressive charter school down a little country lane in Castle Rock, Minnesota. She is the mother of five daughters and lives in Apple Valley, Minnesota with her husband and a crazy springer spaniel named Lois Lane.

ABOUT THE ILLUSTRATOR

Dan McGeehan spent his younger years as an actor, author, playwright, and editor. Now he spends his days drawing, and he is much happier.

TABLE OF CONTENTS

CHAPTER 1

Many Kinds of Weather

What do you do in different kinds of weather? Do you splash in rain puddles or tumble in the snow? On a hot afternoon, do you eat a cold ice cream cone?

You can enjoy nature's weather—rain or shine. Just remember to follow some rules and you'll stay safe.

Hi! I'm Buzz B. Safe. Watch for me! I'll show you how to be safe with weather.

Paying attention to the weather can help you choose the right clothing to wear for the day.

CHAPTER 2

Storm Safety

Rain waters plants and fills rivers, lakes, and streams. But too much rain can cause floods. A river's water can spill over onto the land around it.

Listen to a radio or watch television if heavy rain is falling. You'll find out if there is a flood warning by your home.

If a flood is near, go to higher ground. Do not try to wade or swim in floodwater. You never know how deep the water is. It could be moving faster than you think, too.

Just 6 inches (15 cm) of moving water can knock an adult off their feet.

Sometimes thunder and lightning come along with rain. It's a thunderstorm! A thunderstorm is amazing to see—with its bright flashes and loud cracks. But always watch it from inside a building. If lightning strikes the building, you will still be safe.

A thunderstorm that brings large **hail** and strong winds is a severe thunderstorm. It could even include a **tornado**. This type of weather can **damage** buildings and homes.

If you need to go into the basement, bring a flashlight and a radio with batteries. Grab a game, too. You can play it while you wait for the storm to end. It will be fun, and the time will pass by quickly!

Using a weather radio can be much better than a smartphone during a storm— it doesn't need Internet!

In a severe thunderstorm or tornado, take cover. Go to the lowest level of your home to wait it out. Make sure you stay away from windows.

CHAPTER

3

Hurricanes

Near the ocean, you might see a different kind of storm—a **hurricane**. If a hurricane reaches land, its wild winds can blow trees and signs over. Hurricane winds travel faster than a car travels on a highway. That's why it's important to stay inside a strong building during a hurricane.

During a hurricane, the ocean at the shore can rise about 20 feet (6 m). If this happens, you may have to leave your home until it passes. Your parents will know a safe place where you can go.

Hurricane season in North America is from June 1 to November 30.

CHAPTER 4

Cold Weather Safety

Brr! It's snowing. Do you like to build snowmen in the snow? Make sure you stay warm and cozy. Bundle up with a jacket, snow pants, a scarf, mittens, and boots. And don't forget your hat!

Wearing these things will keep you from getting **frostbite**. When you begin to shiver or feel very tired, it's time for you to go inside and warm up.

It's lots of fun to go sledding in the winter! But remember to play safely. Don't sled on ice or near roads. Have a parent watch you, too.

Symptoms of frostbite include stinging and numbness.

In the US, blizzards are most common in Minnesota, North Dakota, and South Dakota.

14

A **blizzard** usually means school is closed for the day. But ask an adult first if it's safe to play outside.

It's easy to get lost outside during a blizzard. Winds blow at speeds more than 35 miles (56 km) per hour. That's faster than your parent drives his or her car through a small town. The blowing snow makes it hard to see even a few feet in front of you.

Hot Weather Safety

What about when the weather turns **humid** and hot? Do you ride a bike and play tag? It's fun to play outside in summer, but remember a few rules.

Drink lots of cold liquids. Wear clothing that keeps you cool, such as shorts and tank tops. Also, stay in the shade as much as you can.

Swimming in a pool or a lake is a great way to cool off. Just make sure there is an adult to watch you swim. And don't forget to wear sunscreen!

Sunscreens are measured in levels of SPF. That stands for sun protection factor. You should wear a sunscreen with an SPF of at least 30.

STOP

17

Some days it is just too hot! You could get very sick if you ran around outside.

Stay inside your home and keep the air conditioning on. If your home doesn't have air conditioning, spend some time at a cool library reading a good book. Or visit a friend's house and play board games.

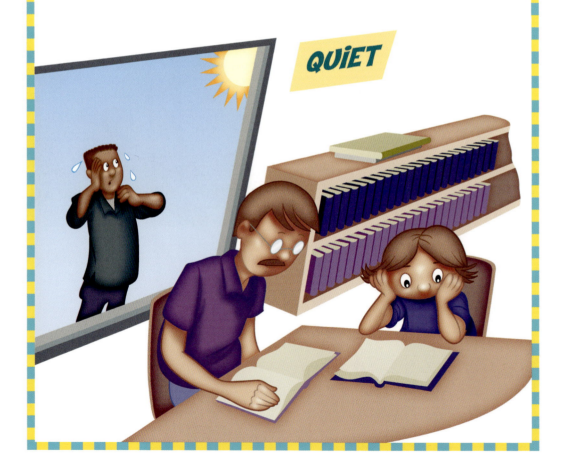

QUIET

TODAY

TOMORROW

SUNNY

RAIN

Your parents can get weather reports on their smartphones, too!

Remember to always keep an eye to the sky. And check out the **weather report** to learn what weather is headed your way. That will keep you safe—indoors and out.

Weather Safety Rules

- Pay attention to the weather report.

- If you hear thunder or see lightning, go inside a house or a building.

- During a tornado or a severe thunderstorm, go to the lowest level of your home and stay away from windows.

- Don't wade or try to swim in flooded areas, including rivers, creeks, or streets.

- In hot weather, drink a lot of water and wear light, loose clothing.

- In cold weather, bundle up!

Wonder More

Wondering about New Information

How much did you know about weather safety before you read this book? What new information did you learn? Write down three new facts that this book taught you. Was the new information surprising? Why or why not?

Wondering How It Matters

Have you ever been affected by very hot or very cold weather? How did you keep your body safe during those times?

Wondering Why

Why is it important to be prepared for different types of weather? Explain your answer.

Ways to Keep Wondering

After reading this book, what questions do you have about weather safety? What can you do to learn more about it?

Make Your Own Rain Gauge
Measure the rain with your own rain gauge!

You will need:
- A clear plastic bottle (a 2-liter soda bottle works well)
- Ruler
- Scissors
- Tape
- Waterproof marker

Instructions:

1. Cut off the top of the bottle. Place it upside down into the bottom half of the bottle. (creating a funnel).

2. Tape the two pieces together. Now use the ruler to mark measurements on the side of the bottle (you can mark inches or centimeters), starting from the bottom.

3. Place the rain gauge outside in an open area where it won't be blocked by trees or buildings. After it rains, measure how much water fell in your area!

Glossary

blizzard (BLIZ-urd): A blizzard is a winter storm with strong wind, heavy snow, and cold temperatures. You may not be able to play outside during a blizzard.

damage (DAM-ij): To damage something means to break or ruin it. A tornado or a hurricane can damage buildings.

frostbite (FRAWST-byt): Frostbite is an injury to the skin caused by cold temperatures. Stay bundled up in cold weather so you don't get frostbite.

hail (HAYL): Hail is small balls of ice that fall from the sky. A severe thunderstorm can bring hail.

humid (HYOO-mid): When the weather is humid, the air feels damp.

hurricane (HUR-uh-kayn): A hurricane is a storm with high winds that forms over an ocean. If a hurricane is coming, you may need to leave your home for safer shelter.

tornado (tor-NAY-doh): A tornado is a spinning tunnel of air that reaches from the clouds to the ground. Take cover in a basement or a strong building during a tornado.

weather report (WETH-ur ri-PORT): A weather report is a news report that tells what the weather will likely be. Listen to or watch the weather report to see if it's okay to play outside.

Find Out More

In the Library

Drimmer, Stephanie Warren. *National Geographic Kids Ultimate Weatherpedia.* Washington, DC: National Geographic, 2019.

Jensen, Belinda. *A Party for Clouds: Thunderstorms.* Minneapolis, MN: Millbrook Press, 2016.

Kostigen, Thomas M. *Extreme Weather: Surviving Tornadoes, Sandstorms, Hailstorms, Blizzards, Hurricanes, and More!* Washington, DC: National Geographic, 2014.

On the Web

Visit our Web site for links about weather safety:
childsworld.com/links

Note to Parents, Teachers, and Librarians: We routinely verify our Web links to make sure they are safe and active sites. So encourage your readers to check them out!

Index